This book belongs to

. . . .

. . . .

A Century of
CHILDREN'S
POEMS

Also compiled by John Foster

Loopy Limericks
Ridiculous Rhymes
Teasing Tongue-Twisters
Dead Funny

A Century of
CHILDREN'S
POEMS

Compiled by John Foster

Illustrated by Emma Shaw-Smith
Silhouette Illustrations by Tim Stevens

An imprint of HarperCollinsPublishers

First published in Great Britain by Collins in 2001
Collins is an imprint of HarperCollins*Publishers* Ltd,
77-85 Fulham Palace Road, Hammersmith
London W6 8JB

The HarperCollins website address is:
www.**fire**and**water**.com

1 3 5 7 9 8 6 4 2

This edition copyright © HarperCollins*Publishers* 2001
Illustrations by Emma Shaw-Smith and Tim Stevens 2001
The acknowledgements on pages 158-160 constitute
an extension of this copyright page.

ISBN 0 00 711251 7

Printed and bound in Great Britain by
Omnia Books Limited
Glasgow

Contents

Poetry Jump-Up

Tell me if ah seeing right
Take a look down de street

Words dancin
words dancin
till dey sweat
words like fishes
jumpin out a net
words wild and free
joinin de poetry revelry
words back to back
words belly to belly

Come on everybody
come and join de poetry band
dis is poetry carnival
dis is poetry bacchanal
when inspiration call
take yu pen in yu hand
if yu dont have a pen
take yu pencil in yu hand
if you don't have a pencil
what the hell
so long de feeling start to swell
just shout de poem out

Words jumpin off de page
tell me if Ah seeing right
words like birds
jumpin out a cage
take a look down de street
words shakin dey waist
words shakin dey bum
words wit black skin
words wit white skin
words wit brown skin
words wit no skin at all
words huggin up words
an saying I want to be a poem today
rhyme or no rhyme
I is a poem today
I mean to have a good time

Words feelin hot hot hot
big words feelin hot hot hot
lil words feelin hot hot hot
even sad words cant help
tappin dey toe
to de riddum of de poetry band

Dis is poetry carnival
dis is poetry bacchanal
so come on everybody
join de celebration
all yu need is plenty perspiration
an a little inspiration
plenty perspiration
an a little inspiration

John Agard

The Old Teacher

There was an old teacher
Who lived in a school,
Slept in the stock-cupboard as a rule,
With sheets of paper to make her bed
And a pillow of hymn-books
Under her head.

There was an old teacher
Who lived for years
In a Wendy house, or so it appears,
Eating the apples the children brought her,
And washing her face
In the goldfish water.

There was an old teacher
Who ended her days
Watching schools' TV and children's plays;
Saving the strength she could just about muster,
To powder her nose
With the blackboard duster.

There was an old teacher
Who finally died
Reading Ginn (Level One), which she couldn't abide.
The words on her tombstone said: TEN OUT OF TEN,
And her grave was the sandpit.
That's all now. Amen.

Allan Ahlberg

Everybody Says

Everybody says
I look just like my mother.
Everybody says
I'm the image of Aunt Bee.
Everybody says
My nose is like my father's
But *I* want to look like *ME*!

Dorothy Aldis

This is a Rune I Have Heard a Tree Say

This is a rune I have heard a tree say:
'Love me. I cannot run away.'

This is a rune I have heard a lark cry:
'So high! But I cannot reach the sky.'

This is a rune I have heard a dog bark:
'I see what is not even there in the dark.'

This is a rune I have heard a fish weep:
'I am trying to find you when I leap.'

This is a rune I have heard a cat miaow:
'I died eight times so be kind to me now.'

This is a rune I have heard a man say:
'Hold your head up and you see far away.'

George Barker

Rebecca

Who Slammed Doors for Fun and Perished Miserably

A Trick that everyone abhors
In Little Girls is slamming Doors.
A Wealthy Banker's Little Daughter
Who lived in Palace Green, Bayswater
(By name Rebecca Offendort),
Was given to this Furious Sport.

She would deliberately go
And Slam the door like Billy-Ho!
To make her Uncle Jacob start.
She was not really bad at heart,
But only rather rude and wild;
She was an aggravating child.

It happened that a Marble Bust
Of Abraham was standing just
Above the Door this little Lamb
Had carefully prepared to Slam,
And Down it came! It knocked her flat!
It laid her out! She looked like that!

★ ★ ★ ★ ★ ★ ★ ★

Her Funeral Sermon (which was long
And followed by a Sacred Song)
Mentioned her Virtues, it is true,
But dwelt upon her Vices, too,
And showed the Dreadful End of One
Who goes and slams the Door for Fun.

Hilaire Belloc

The Hobby Horse

The hobby horse lies forgotten in the attic;
The uncle who made the beautiful hobby horse is far
    away;
The boy who rode the horse, tugging the reins as the
    wild mane flowed in the wind, has grown up.
The uncle who carved the noble wooden head is far, far
    away.
The toy horse lies forsaken in the attic.

But listen!
Can you hear the distant thunder of hooves?

Gerard Benson

Benediction

Thanks to the ear
that someone may hear.

Thanks to seeing
that someone may see.

Thanks to feeling
that someone may feel.

Thanks to touch
that one may be touched.

Thanks to flowering of white moon
and spreading shawl of black night
holding villages and cities together.

James Berry

Visit to de Dentist

Wat a likkle cry baby!
Look ow de bwoy a bawl,
One likkle injection im get
Im no ha no shame at all.

Ah bet im older dan mi, Mama,
But mi wouldn' cry so loud,
In fac' mi wouldn' cry at all
Especially eena crowd.

An look ow people a look pon im,
Mi shame fi im yuh see,
Mi couldn' show mi face agen
Ef dat likkle bwoy was mi.

Eh eh, but look noh, Mama,
One nedda one a cry,
An de gal who a come out deh now
Wata full up har yeye.

But faba someting really wrong
Else dem wouldn' frighten soh,
Mama, guess wha happen,
Mi toothache gone, yuh know.

De nurse a call wi, mama,
But a couldn' fi mi time a'ready?
'Ladies before gentlemen'
Mek da gal yah go before mi.

She go a'ready? A mi one lef?
Nurse, tell de dentist noh fe badda,
Mi toothache gone fi good now.
Unless im wan' fe see mi madda?

Mama, yuh wouldn' force mi,
An know ow mi fraid a needle to?
No badda cyah mi een deh
Waia! Smaddy come help mi do!

Waia! Murder! Help! Police!
No mek im touch mi oh!
Mi heart no too good, doctor,
Mi wi dead from fright yuh know.

Wait, Mama, yuh hear dat?
Im cyan do nutten when mi gum swell soh,
So mi mus tek some aspirin tonight
An come back come see im tomorrow.

Dis dentist is a nice man,
Im smile so sweet an warm
Wha mek dem pickney cry, cry soh?
Im wouldn' do dem no harm.

Watch dat dey one still a bawl
De pickney no hab no shame
Mi woulda nebba mek so much nize.
(Mi glad mi get whey teday all de same.)

Valerie Bloom

Jim

There never was a nicer boy
Than Mrs Jackson's Jim.
The sun should drop its greatest gold
On him.

Because, when Mother-dear was sick,
He brought her cocoa in.
And brought her broth, and brought her bread.
And brought her medicine.

And, tipping, tidied up her room.
And would not let her see
He missed his game of baseball
Terribly.

Gwendolyn Brooks

The Secret Song

Who saw the petals
  drop from the rose?
I, said the spider,
But nobody knows.

Who saw the sunset
  flash on a bird?
I, said the fish,
But nobody heard.

Who saw the fog
  come over the sea?
I, said the sea pigeon,
Only me.

Who saw the first
  green light of the sun?
I, said the night owl,
The only one.

Who saw the moss
  creep over the stone?
I, said the gray fox,
All alone.

Margaret Wise Brown

Who?

Who is that child I see wandering, wandering
Down by the side of the quivering stream?
Why does he seem not to hear, though I call to him?
Where does he come from, and what is his name?

Why do I see him at sunrise and sunset
Taking, in old-fashioned clothes, the same track?
Why, when he walks, does he cast not a shadow
Though the sun rises and falls at his back?

Why does the dust lie so thick on the hedgerow
By the great field where a horse pulls the plough?
Why do I see only meadows, where houses
Stand in a line by the riverside now?

Why does he move like a wraith by the water,
Soft as the thistledown on the breeze blown?
When I draw near him so that I may hear him,
Why does he say that his name is my own?

Charles Causley

About the Teeth of Sharks

The thing about a shark is – teeth,
One row above, one row beneath.

Now take a close look. Do you find
It has another row behind?

Still closer – here, I'll hold your hat:
Has it a third row behind that?

Now look in and... Look out! Oh my,
I'll *never* know now! Well, goodbye.

John Ciardi

Mushrooms

Secret as toads. After a night's rain,
rise with the sun, dawn's flush on pillar and dome;
stronger than daisied turf, push into the light,
swell in an hour, tight, complete.
Summer's late harvest, miracles of white,
button up meadows, cool in the hill folds,
older than caveman wandering his wilderness.
Nothing more holy, live with manna's touch,
they shine, dew-crowned and comfortable.
And then, before final cockcrow fades,
ungathered and overblown in every hiding place,
wearily topple over on blackened stalks,
drenched with decay, worms in the soggy flesh.
By afternoon, dwindled to dust,
the mystery gone with the dew.

Leonard Clark

Country Barnyard

Cats and kittens, kittens and cats
under the barn and under the shed;
a face by the steps, a tail by the ramp
and off they go, if they hear a tread!

Sleep in the sun with one eye on guard,
doze in the grass with a listening ear,
run for the darkness under the barn
as soon as a human being draws near!

Not quite wild and not quite tame,
thin and limber, with hungry eye:
the house cat sits at the kitchen door
disdainfully watching her kin go by.

Elizabeth Coatsworth

Spider

I'm told that the spider
Has coiled up inside her
Enough silky material
To spin an aerial
One-way track
To the moon and back;
Whilst I
Cannot even catch a fly.

Frank Collymore

Bluebells

This year and every year
The long-legged trees
Stand, now Spring is here,
In a bright blue sea.

No one can count the bluebells
That gather together
Until they fill
The woods with waves of their colour.

Beneath new shining leaves
On the long-legged trees
Children gathering flowers
Paddle in a bluebell sea.

Stanley Cook

Huff

I am in a tremendous huff –
Really, really bad.
It isn't any ordinary huff –
It's one of the best I've had.

I plan to keep it up for a month
Or maybe for a year
And you needn't think you can make me smile
Or talk to you. No fear.

I can do without you and her and them –
Too late to make amends.
I'll think deep thoughts on my own for a while,
Then find some better friends.

And they'll be wise and kind and good
And bright enough to see
That they should behave with proper respect
Towards somebody like me.

I do like being in a huff –
Cold fury is so heady.
I've been like this for half an hour
And it's cheered me up already.

Perhaps I'll give them another chance,
Now I'm feeling stronger
But they'd better watch out – my next big huff
Could last much, much, much longer.

Wendy Cope

Aunt Sponge and Aunt Spiker

'I look and smell,' Aunt Sponge declared, 'as lovely as a rose
Just feast your eyes upon my face, observe my shapely nose
Behold my heavenly silky locks!
And if I take off both my socks
You'll see my dainty toes.'
'But don't forget,' Aunt Spiker cried, 'how much your
      tummy shows!'

Aunt Sponge went red. Aunt Spiker said, 'My sweet,
      you cannot win,
Behold MY gorgeous curvy shape, my teeth,
      my charming grin!
Oh, beauteous me! How I adore
My radiant looks! And please ignore
The pimple on my chin.'
'My dear old trout!' Aunt Sponge cried out. 'You're only
      bones and skin!

'Such loveliness as I possess can only truly shine
In Hollywood!' Aunt Sponge declared. 'Oh, wouldn't
    that be fine!
I'd capture all the nations' hearts!
They'd give me all the leading parts!
The stars would all resign!'
'I think you'd make,' Aunt Spiker said, 'a lovely
Frankenstein.'

Roald Dahl

The Listeners

'Is there anybody there?' said the Traveller,
  Knocking on the moonlit door;
And his horse in the silence champed the grasses
  Of the forest's ferny floor:
And a bird flew up out of the turret,
  Above the Traveller's head:
And he smote upon the door again a second time;
  'Is there anybody there?' he said.
But no one descended to the Traveller;
  No head from the leaf-fringed sill
Leaned over and looked into his grey eyes,

Where he stood perplexed and still.
But only a host of phantom listeners
   That dwelt in the lone house then
Stood listening in the quiet of the moonlight
   To that voice from the world of men:
Stood thronging the faint moonbeams on the dark stair,
   That goes down to the empty hall,
Hearkening in an air stirred and shaken
   By the lonely Traveller's call.
And he felt in his heart their strangeness,
   Their stillness answering his cry,
While his horse moved, cropping the dark turf,
   'Neath the starred and leafy sky;
For he suddenly smote on the door, even
   Louder, and lifted his head:–
'Tell them I came, and no one answered,
   That I kept my word,' he said.
Never the least stir made the listeners,
   Though every word he spake
Fell echoing through the shadowiness of the still house
   From the one man left awake:
Ay, they heard his foot upon the stirrup,
   And the sound of iron on stone,
And how the silence surged softly backward,
   When the plunging hoofs were gone.

Walter de la Mare

I'm Frightened in Dark Caves

their blackness drowns
and oozes into my skin
with the chill of deep earth.

They take up echoes
and wring them like living things
and fling them
so they scuttle to hiding-holes
and leave their wetness
dripping like blood over me

and weight of rock on rock on rock
bears down to crush my breath
and all light's lost.
I stumble on like a blind beast
into nothingness.

Last year a cave's throat
belched out screaming gulls
that tore my hair
and beat their wings around my face
and spewed my shouts and theirs
out into air again.

Into lovely air.

Berlie Doherty

Chocs

Into the half-pound box of Moonlight
my small hand crept.
There was an electrifying rustle.
There was a dark and glamorous scent.
Into my open, moist mouth
the first Montelimar went.

Down in the crinkly second layer,
five finger-piglets snuffled
among the Hazelnut Whirl,
the Caramel Square,
the Black Cherry and Almond Truffle.

Bliss.

I chomped. I gorged.
I stuffed my face,
till only the Coffee Cream
was left for the owner of the box –
tough luck, Anne Pope –
oh, and half an Orange Supreme.

Carol Ann Duffy

Misnomer

Once I ate a jellyfish–
it didn't taste like jelly;
it didn't even taste of fish–
but oh my aching belly.

Michael Dugan

The Rainflower

Down in the forest where light never falls
There's a place that no one else knows,
A deep marshy hollow beside a grey lake
And that's where the rainflower grows.

The one silver rainflower that's left in the world,
Alone in the mist and the damp,
Lifts up its bright head from a cluster of leaves
And shines through the gloom like a lamp.

Far from the footpaths and far from the roads,
In a silence where no birds call,
It blooms like a secret, a star in the dark,
The last silver rainflower of all.

So keep close behind me and follow me down,
I'll take you where no one else goes,
And there in the hollow beside the grey lake,
We'll stand where the rainflower grows.

Richard Edwards

The song of the Jellicles

Jellicle Cats come out tonight
Jellicle Cats come one come all:
The Jellicle Moon is shining bright –
Jellicles come to the Jellicle Ball.

Jellicle Cats are black and white,
Jellicle Cats are rather small;
Jellicle Cats are merry and bright,
And pleasant to hear when they caterwaul.
Jellicle Cats have cheerful faces,
Jellicle Cats have bright black eyes;
They like to practise their airs and graces
And wait for the Jellicle Moon to rise.

Jellicle Cats develop slowly,
Jellicle Cats are not too big;
Jellicle Cats are roly-ploy,
They know how to dance a gavotte and a jig.
Until the Jellicle Moon appears
They make their toilette and take their repose:
Jellicles wash behind their ears,
Jellicles dry between their toes.

Jellicle Cats are white and black,
Jellicle Cats are of moderate size;
Jellicles jump like a jumping-jack,
Jellicle Cats have moonlit eyes.
They're quiet enough in the morning hours,
They're quiet enough in the afternoon,
Reserving their terpsichorean powers
To dance by the light of the Jellicle Moon.

Jellicle Cats are black and white,
Jellicle Cats (as I said) are small;
If it happens to be a stormy night
They will practise a caper or two in the hall.
If it happens the sun is shining bright
You would say they had nothing to do at all:
They are resting and saving themselves to be right
For the Jellicle Moon and the Jellicle Ball.

T.S. Eliot

The Weather

What's the weather on about?
Why is the rain so down on us?
Why does the sun glare at us so?

Why does the hail dance so prettily?
Why is the snow such an overall?
Why is the wind such a tearaway?

Why is the mud so fond of our feet?
Why is the ice so keen to upset us?
Who does the weather think it is?

Gavin Ewart

Zodiac

What are the Signs of Zodiac,
Marked in stars on Heaven's track?

The Water-Carrier bears on high,
His jar in January's sky.

February brings a pair
Of Fish to swim in dark blue air.

In March a horned Ram doth run
Between the visits of the sun.

April rides upon a Bull
Vigorous and beautiful.

The Twins we call the Gemini
May-month cradles in the sky.

In June the Crab goes crawling o'er
The spaces of the heavenly shore.

Where the Crab no longer creeps,
In July the Lion leaps.

Through August night, like daisy-laden
Meadows, walks a Vestal Maiden.

September, though it blows big gales,
Holds aloft a pair of Scales.

On October's map is shown
A star-bespangled Scorpion.

In November, kneeling low,
See, the Archer bends his bow.

December's frolic is a Goat
Bleating in his starry throat.

These are the Signs of Zodiac,
Marking time on Heaven's track.

Eleanor Farjeon

'Jump over the moon?'
the cow declared

'Jump over the moon?' the cow declared,
  'With a dish and a spoon. Not me.
I need a suit and a rocket ship
  And filmed by the BBC.

'I want a roomy capsule stall
  For when I blast away,
And an astronaut as a dairymaid
  And a bale of meadow hay.'

She gave a twitch of her lazy rump,
  'Space travel takes up time.
I certainly don't intend to jump
  For a mad old nursery rhyme.'

Max Fatchen

Something Told the Wild Geese

Something told the wild geese
It was time to go,
Though the fields lay golden
Something whispered, 'Snow!'
Leaves were green and stirring,
Berries lustre-glossed,
But beneath warm feathers
Something cautioned, 'Frost!'

All the sagging orchards
Steamed with amber spice,
But each wild beast stiffened
At remembered ice.
Something told the wild geese
It was time to fly –
Summer sun was on their wings,
Winter in their cry.

Rachel Field

Christmas Secrets

Secrets long and secrets wide,
brightly wrapped and tightly tied,

Secrets fat and secrets thin,
boxed and sealed and hidden in,

Some that rattle, some that squeak,
some that caution, 'Do Not Peek'...

Hurry, Christmas, get here first,
get here fast... before we *burst*.

Aileen Fisher

Horrible Things

'What's the horriblest thing you've seen?'
said Nell to Jean.

'Some grey-coloured, trodden-on Plasticine;
On a plate, a left-over cold baked bean;
A cloakroom ticket numbered thirteen;
A slice of meat without any lean;
The smile of a spiteful fairy-tale queen;
A thing in the sea like a brown submarine;
A cheese fur-coated in brilliant green;
A bluebottle perched on a piece of sardine.
What's the horriblest thing *you've* seen?'
Said Jean to Nell.

'Your face, as you tell
Of all the horriblest things you've seen.'

Roy Fuller

Witch, Witch

'Witch, witch, where do you fly?'…
'Under the clouds and over the sky.'

'Witch, witch, what do you eat?'…
'Little black apples from Hurricane Street.'

'Witch, witch, what do you drink?'…
'Vinegar, blacking and good red ink.'

'Witch, witch, where do you sleep?'…
'Up in the clouds where pillows are cheap.'

Rose Fyleman

mattie lou at twelve

they always said 'what a pretty little girl you are'
and she would smile

they always said 'how nice of you to help
your mother with your brothers and sisters'
and she would smile and think

they said 'what lovely pigtails you have
and you plaited them all by yourself!'
and she would say 'thank you'

and they always said 'all those Bs
what a good student you are'
and she would smile and say 'thank you'

they said 'you will make a fine woman some day'
and she would smile and go her way

because she knew

Nikki Giovanni

The Sprat and the Jackfish

'Who cares if it's fair?'
the jackfish said,
flicking its fin,
flashing its head.

'It's nothing to me
that you found it first;
it's mine to keep
though you cry till you burst.'

The small sprat flapped
its silver tail
and thought, 'I wish
I were a whale.

I'd swallow this jackfish
with one gulp;
its body I would
turn to pulp.

Because you're just that much
bigger than me,
you think you 're the ruler
of the sea!

Well, take my worm
it's yours all right –
in this unfair world
it's might that's right.'

'It's a juicy worm!'
the jackfish said,
flicking its fin,
flashing its head.

Then, choking and twisting,
tormented, it sped
along an invisible
line overhead…

But the sprat did not see
as it went on its way
'It's an unfair world,'
was all it could say.

Grace Walker Gordon

Inconsiderate Hannah

Naughty little Hannah said
She could make her Grandma whistle,
So, that night, inside her bed,
Placed some nettles and a thistle.

Though dear Grandma quite infirm is,
Heartless Hannah watched her settle,
With her poor old epidermis
Resting up against a nettle.

Suddenly she reached the thistle!
My! you should have heard her whistle.

★ ★ ★ ★ ★ ★ ★ ★

A successful plan was Hannah's
But I cannot praise her manners.

Harry Graham

A Song for Toad

The world has held great Heroes,
  As history-books have showed;
But never a name to go down to fame
  Compared to that of Toad!

The clever men at Oxford
  Know all that there is to be knowed.
But they none of them know one half as much
  As intelligent Mr Toad!

The animals sat in the ark and cried,
  Their tears in torrents flowed.
Who was it said, 'There's land ahead'?
  Encouraging Mr Toad!

The Army all saluted
  As they marched along the road.
Was it the King? Or Kitchener?
  No. It was Mr Toad.

The Queen and her ladies-in-waiting
  Sat at the window and sewed.
She cried, 'Look! Who's that *handsome* man?'
  They answered, 'Mr Toad.'

The motor-car went Poop-poop-poop
　　As it raced along the road.
Who was it steered it into a pond?
　　Ingenious Mr Toad!

Kenneth Grahame

The Penny Fiddle

Yesterday I bought a penny fiddle
　　And put it to my chin to play,
But I found that the strings were painted,
　　So I threw my fiddle away.

A gipsy girl found my penny fiddle
　　As it lay abandoned there;
When she asked me if she might keep it,
　　I told her I did not care.

Then she drew such music from the fiddle
　　With help of a farthing bow,
That I offered five shillings for the secret.
　　But, alas, she would not let it go.

Robert Graves

Trick of the Lights

Late, late at night
you may never get home. They wink the word
from light to light

all down the long straight
empty road. Each one in turn will turn
against you, but they wait

green as grass on the opposite side
of a triptrap bridge, where amber teeth
and bloodshot eyes might hide

as you pedal for home, too fast. Too late.

Philip Gross

The Dolls

'Whenever you dress me dolls, mammy,
   Why do you dress them so,
And make them gallant soldiers,
   When never a one I know;
And not as gentle ladies
   With frills and frocks and curls,
As people dress the dollies
   Of other little girls?'

Ah – why did she not answer: –
   'Because your mammy's heed
Is always gallant soldiers,
   As well may be, indeed.
One of them was your daddy,
   His name I must not tell;
He's not the dad who lives here,
   But one I love too well.'

Thomas Hardy

Trout

Hangs, a fat gun-barrel,
deep under arched bridges
or slips like butter down
the throat of the river.

From the depths smooth-skinned as plums
his muzzle gets bull's eye;
picks off grass-seed and moths
that vanish, torpedoed.

Where water unravels
over gravel-bed he
is fired from the shallows
white belly reporting

flat; darts like a tracer-
bullet back between stones
and is never burnt out.
A volley of cold blood

ramrodding the current.

Seamus Heaney

The Haunted Disco

When it's half past three in the morning
right through to break of day,
a phantom DJ opens up
for the dead to come and play.

The coloured lights are flashing,
and the crowd are on their feet,
but there's no sound of them dancing
to the ghostly disco-beat.

When there's ice between your shoulders,
and the hairs rise on your neck,
and you don't know who you're dancing with
at the haunted discotheque.

When you daren't look at your partner,
and you fear their bony hand,
the go-go ghosts all boogie
to an ancient, nameless band.

The graveyard sounds are all around
the mist drifts everywhere,
but the ghastly crowds in mini-shrouds
rave on without a care.

When there's ice between your shoulders,
and the hairs rise on your neck,
and you know you'll dance for ever
at the haunted discotheque.

Adrian Henri

The Fox

It was twenty years ago I saw the fox
Gliding along the edge of prickling corn,
A nefarious shadow
Between the emerald field and bristling hedge,
On velvet feet he went.

The wind was kind, withheld from him my scent
Till my threaded gaze unmasked him standing there,
The colour of last year's beech-leaves, pointed black,
Poised, uncertain, quivering nose aware
Of danger throbbing through each licking leaf.
One foot uplifted, balanced on the brink
Of perennial fear, the hunter hunted stood.

I heard no alien stir in the friendly wood,
But the fox's sculpted attitude was tense
With scenting, listening, with a seventh sense
Flaring to the alert; I heard no sound
Threaten the morning; and followed his amber stare,
But in that hair-breadth moment, that flick of the eye,
He vanished.

And now, whenever I hear the expectant cry
Of hounds on the empty air,
I look to a gap in the hedge and see him there
Filling the space with fear; the trembling leaves
Are frozen in his stillness till I hear
His leashed-up breathing – how the stretch of time
Contracts within the flash of re-creation!

Phoebe Hesketh

Homework

Homework sits on top of Sunday, squashing Sunday flat.
Homework has the smell of Monday, homework's very fat
Heavy books and piles of paper, answers I don't know.
Sunday evening's almost finished, now I'm going to go
Do my homework in the kitchen. Maybe just a snack.
Then I'll sit right down and start as soon as I run back
For some chocolate sandwich cookies. Then I'll really do
All that homework in a minute. First I'll see what new
Show they've got on television in the living room.
Everybody's laughing there, but misery and gloom
And a full refrigerator are where I am at.
I'll just have another sandwich. Homework's very fat.

Russell Hoban

Brother

I had a little brother
And I brought him to my mother
And I said I want another
Little brother for a change.
But she said don't be a bother
So I took him to my father
And I said this little bother
Of a brother's very strange.

But he said one little brother
Is exactly like another
And every little brother
Misbehaves a bit he said.
So I took the little bother
From my mother and my father
And I put the little bother
Of a brother back to bed.

Mary Ann Hoberman

Mother to Son

Well, son, I'll tell you:
Life for me ain't been no crystal stair.
It's had tacks in it,
And splinters,
And boards torn up,
And places with no carpet on the floor—
Bare.
But all the time
I'se been a climbin' on,
And reachin' landin's,
and turnin' corners,
And sometimes goin' in the dark
Where there ain't been no light.
So boy, don't you turn back.
Don't you set down on the steps
'Cause you finds it's kinder hard.
Don't you fall now—
For I'se still goin', honey,
I'se still climbin',
And life for me ain't been no crystal stair.

Langston Hughes

There Came a Day

There came a day that caught the summer
Wrung its neck
Plucked it
And ate it.

Now what shall I do with the trees?
The day said, the day said.
Strip them bare, strip them bare.
Let's see what is really there.

And what shall I do with the sun?
The day said, the day said.
Roll him away till he's cold and small.
He'll come back rested if he comes back at all.

And what shall I do with the birds?
The day said, the day said.
The birds I've frightened, let them flit,
I'll hang out pork for the brave tomtit.

And what shall I do with the seed?
The day said, the day said.
Bury it deep, see what it's worth.
See if it can stand the earth.

What shall I do with the people?
The day said, the day said.
Stuff them with apple and blackberry pie –
They'll love me then till the day they die.

There came this day and he was autumn.
His mouth was wide
And red as a sunset.
His tail was an icicle.

Ted Hughes

Friends

I fear it's very wrong of me,
And yet I must admit,
When someone offers friendship
I want the *whole* of it.
I don't want everybody else
To share my friends with me.
At least, I want *one* special one,
Who, indisputably,

Likes me much more than all the rest,
Who's always on my side,
Who never cares what others say,
Who lets me come and hide
Within his shadow, in his house –
It doesn't matter where –
Who lets me simply be myself,
Who's always, *always* there.

Elizabeth Jennings

November Returns

Firework time, and this year, gales.
Large trees dip and bow tearing their leaves
Against the air, which seems to thicken now.
Not a quiet time even when the weather is quiet.
Fireworks, and your birthday: the year beginning
Apart from the calendar. A time when things have
    happened.
Advenire, Advent: to come to reach to happen.

Some years there is sunshine pale in woods.
It lies in splashes like paint on leaves, on the track,
A pausing in the year before it swings
Down to the dark,
And the leaves thin – beech-gold, pebble-brown
A clearing in the grove.
On some dim soft dun afternoon
Having to wait for something, you go a stroll
At the back of the works ('back in twenty minutes').
An astounding tree picked out by secret sunshine
Makes sense of the Golden Bough, the magic in woods.

Bonfires, Hallowe'en past, children running
    through streets,
Something stirring in the blood that makes us rise
And stand at the window, leaving the curtain ajar,
Expectant of something, watching waiting
For something to happen; someone, perhaps, to
    arrive.
Maybe it is just the wind shifting direction
Dropping leaves at doors, pattering rain on the
    windows.

I draw the curtains, light the fire, for you
And others I have lit for at this time:
Ghosts returning to their winter quarters
To keep me company, to celebrate the season.

Jenny Joseph

Big Hole

My best friend Jenny Colquhoun has moved on.
She's gone to live in a posher part of town.
She left a big hole; an empty space next to my desk.
My hands hold themselves on the way to school.

But see in her new house she has a dining room,
a TV room – imagine a room just for watching! –
and her own bedroom. I stayed the night;
got lost on my way back from the bathroom.

I was there the day before her ninth birthday.
I was the special friend from the old school.
But when her new friends came they stared
till I thought I should check the mirror, as if

I had a big hole in my tights. 'What did *you*
get Jenny for her birthday?' '*Anne of Green Gables*'
I said, burning under the wrong dress,
wanting the thick carpet to swallow me up.

'Have you always been that colour?' says the one
with the freckles. And a giggle spreads from room
to room till Jenny's beautiful red-haired mother
saves me: '*Ann of Green Gables*? A wonderful book.'

Jackie Kay

Whose Boo is Whose?

Two ghosts I know once traded heads
And shrieked and shook their sheets to shreds –
'You're me!' yelled one, 'and me, I'm you!
Now who can boo the loudest boo?'

'Me!' cried the other, and for proof
He booed a boo that scared the roof
Right off our house. The TV set
Jumped higher than a jumbo jet.

The first ghost snickered. 'Why, you creep,
Call that a boo? That feeble beep?
Hear *this*!' – and sucking in a blast
Of wind, he puffed his sheet so vast

And booed so hard, a passing goose
Lost all its down. The moon shook loose
And fell and smashed to smithereens –
Stars scattered like spilled jellybeans.

'How's that for booing, boy? I win,'
Said one. The other scratched a chin
Where only bone was – 'Win or lose?
How can we tell whose boo is whose?'

X. J. Kennedy

The Way Through the Woods

They shut the road through the woods
Seventy years ago.
Weather and rain have undone it again,
And now you would never know
There was once a road through the woods
Before they planted the trees.
It is underneath the coppice and heath
And the thin anemones.
Only the keeper sees
That, where the ring-dove broods,
And the badgers roll at ease,
There was once a road through the woods.

Yet, if you enter the woods
Of a summer evening late,
When the night-air cools on the trout-ringed pools
Where the otter whistles his mate,
(They fear not men in the woods,
Because they see so few.)
You will hear the beat of a horse's feet,
And the swish of a skirt in the dew,
Steadily cantering through
The misty solitudes,
As though they perfectly knew
The old lost road through the woods...
But there is no road through the woods.

Rudyard Kipling

Thunder and Lightning

Blood punches through every vein
As lightning strips the windowpane.

Under its flashing whip, a white
Village leaps to light.

On tubs of thunder, fists of rain
Slog it out of sight again.

Blood punches the heart with fright
As rain belts the village night.

James Kirkup

Rules

Do not jump on ancient uncles.
*

Do not yell at average mice.
*

Do not wear a broom to breakfast.
*

Do not ask a snake's advice.
*

Do not bathe in chocolate pudding.
*

Do not talk to bearded bears.
*

Do not smoke cigars on sofas.
*

Do not dance on velvet chairs.
*

Do not take a whale to visit
Russell's mother's cousin's yacht.
*

And whatever else you do do
It is better you
Do not.

Karla Kuskin

Cold Feet

They have all gone across
They are all turning to see
They are all shouting 'come on'
They are all waiting for me.

I look through the gaps in the footway
And my heart shrivels with fear,
For far below the river is flowing
So quick and so cold and so clear.

And all that there is between it
And me falling down there is this:
A few wooden planks not very thick –
And between each, a little abyss.

The holes get right under my sandals.
I can see straight through to the rocks,
And if I don't look, I can feel it,
Just there, through my shoes and my socks.

Suppose my feet and my legs withered up
And slipped through the slats like a rug?
Suppose I suddenly went very thin
Like the baby that slid down the plug?

I know that it cannot happen
But suppose that it did, what then?
Would they be able to find me
And take me back home again?

They have all gone across
They are all waiting to see
They are all shouting 'come on' –
But they'll have to carry me.

Brian Lee

The Butterfly

Butterfly,
    butterfly,
life's a
    dream;

all that we
    see,
and all that we
    seem,

here for a
    jiffy
and then
    goodbye—

butterfly,
    butterfly,
flutter
    on by.

Dennis Lee

Balloons...Balloons

Balloons, balloons
    on coloured string
    are blowing out
    into the Spring.

Balloons, balloons
    filled up with air
    are sailing off
    to everywhere.

Balloons, balloons
    all bright and round
    are floating up
    without a sound

Myra Cohn Livingston

The Ass's Song

In a nearby town
there lived an Ass,

who in this life
(as all good asses do)

helped his master,
loved his master,

served his master,
faithfully and true.

Now the good Ass worked
the whole day through,

from dawn to dusk
(and on his Sundays, too)

so the master knew
as he rode to mass

God let him sit
on the perfect Ass.

When the good Ass died
and fled above

for his reward
(that all good asses have)

his master made
from his loyal hide

a whip with which
his successor was lashed.

Christopher Logue

The Huntsman

Kagwa hunted the lion,
  Through bush and forest went his spear.
One day he found the skull of a man
  And said to it, 'How did you come here?'
The skull opened its mouth and said,
  'Talking brought me here.'

Kagwa hurried home;
  Went to the king's chair and spoke:
'In the forest I found a talking skull.'
  The king was silent. Then he said slowly,
'Never since I was born of my mother
  Have I seen or heard of a skull which spoke.'

The king called out his guards:
  'Two of you now go with him
And find this talking skull;
  But if his tale is a lie
And the skull speaks no word,
  This Kagwa himself must die.'

They rode into the forest;
  For days and nights they found nothing.
At last they saw the skull; Kagwa
  Said to it, 'How did you come here?'
The skull said nothing. Kagwa implored,
  But the skull said nothing.

The guards said, 'Kneel down.'
  They killed him with sword and spear.
Then the skull opened its mouth;
  'Huntsman, how did you come here?'
And the dead man answered,
  'Talking brought me here.'

Edward Lowbury

The Star in the Pail

I took the pail for water when the sun was high
And I left it in the shadow of the barn nearby.

When evening slippered over like the moth's brown wing,
I went to fetch the water from the cool wellspring.

The night was clear and warm and wide, and I alone
Was walking by the light of stars as thickly sown

As wheat across the prairie, or the first fall flakes,
Or spray upon the lawn – the kind the sprinkler makes.

But every star was far away as far can be,
With all the starry silence sliding over me.

And every time I stopped I set the pail down slow,
For when I stooped to pick the handle up to go

Of all the stars in heaven there was one to spare,
And he silvered in the water and I left him there.

David McCord

Cross Porpoises

The porpoises
were looking really cross
so I went over
and talked at them

Soon they cheered up
and swam away
leaving laughter-bubbles
in their wake

It never fails,
talking at cross porpoises.

Roger McGough

The Pines

Hear the rumble,
Oh, hear the crash.
The great trees tumble.
The strong boughs smash.

Men with saws
Are cutting the pines –
That marched like soldiers
In straight green lines.

Seventy years
Have made them tall.
It takes ten minutes
To make them fall.

And breaking free
With never a care,
The pine cones leap
Through the clear, bright air.

Margaret Mahy

Sea-Fever

I must go down to the seas again, to the lonely sea and
   the sky,
And all I ask is a tall ship and a star to steer her by,
And the wheel's kick and the wind's song and the white
   sail's shaking,
And a grey mist on the sea's face and a grey dawn
   breaking.

I must go down to the seas again, for the call of the
   running tide
Is a wild call and a clear call that may not be denied;
And all I ask is a windy day with the white clouds
   flying,
And the flung spray and the blown spume, and the
   sea-gulls crying.

I must go down to the seas again, to the vagrant gypsy
   life,
To the gull's way and the whale's way where the wind's
   like a whetted knife;
And all I ask is a merry yarn from a laughing fellow-
   rover,
And quiet sleep and a sweet dream when the long trick's
   over.

John Masefield

Fantasia

I dream
of
giving birth
to
a child
who will ask,
'Mother,
what was war?'

Eve Merriam

The ABC

'Twas midnight in the schoolroom
And every desk was shut,
When suddenly from the alphabet
Was heard a lout 'Tut-tut!'

Said A to B, 'I don't like C;
His manners are a lack.
For all I ever see of C
Is a semi-circular back!'

'I disagree,' said D to B,
'I've never found C so.
From where I stand, he seems to be
An uncompleted O.'

C was vexed, 'I'm much perplexed,
You criticize my shape.
I'm made like that, to help spell Cat
And Cow and Cool and Cape.'

'He's right,' said E; said F, 'Whoopee!'
Said G, ''Ip, 'ip, 'ooray!'
'You're dropping me,' roared H to G.
'Don't do it please I pray!'

'Out of my way,' LL said to K.
I'll make poor I look ILL.'
To stop this stunt, J stood in front,
And presto! ILL was JILL.

'U know,' said V, 'that W
Is twice the age of me,
For as a Roman V is five
I'm half as young as he.'

X and Y yawned sleepily,
'Look at the time!' they said.
'Let's all get off to beddy byes.'
They did, then, 'Z–z–z.'

or

alternative last verse

X and Y yawned sleepily,
'Look at the time!' they said.
They all jumped in to beddy byes
And the last one in was Z!

Spike Milligan

89

Forgiven

I found a little beetle, so that Beetle was his name,
And I called him Alexander and he answered just the same
I put him in a match-box, and I kept him all the day...
And Nanny let my beetle out –

 Yes, Nanny let my beetle out –

 She went and let my beetle out –

 And Beetle ran away.

She said she didn't mean it, and I never said she did,
She said she wanted matches and she just took off the lid,
She said that she was sorry, but it's difficult to catch
An excited sort of beetle you've mistaken for a match.

She said that she was sorry, and I really mustn't mind,
As there's lots and lots of beetles which she's certain we
    could find,
If we looked about the garden for the holes where beetles
    hid –
And we'd get another match-box and write BEETLE on
    the lid.

We went to all the places which a beetle might be near,
And we made the sort of noises which a beetle likes to hear,
And I saw a kind of something, and I gave a sort of shout:
'A beetle-house and Alexander Beetle is coming out!'

It was Alexander Beetle I'm as certain as can be,
And he had a sort of look as if he thought it must be Me,
And he had a sort of look as if he thought he ought to say:
'I'm very very sorry that I tried to run away.'

And Nanny's very sorry too for you-know-what-she-did,
And she's writing ALEXANDER very blackly on the lid.
So Nan and Me are friends, because it's difficult to catch
An excited Alexander you've mistaken for a match.

A.A. Milne

Nobody Rides the Unicorn

His coat is like snowflakes
Woven with silk.
When he goes galloping
He flows like milk.

His life is all gentle
And his heart is bold.
His single horn is magical
Barley sugar gold.

Nobody rides the Unicorn
As he grazes under a secret sun.
His understanding is so great
That he forgives us, every one.

Nobody rides the Unicorn,
His mind is peaceful as the grass.
He is the loveliest one of all
And he sleeps behind the waterfall.

Adrian Mitchell

Mr Cartwright's Counting Rhyme

One, two
You, boy, yes I'm talking to you

three, four
I've wiped the floor

five, six
with others of your kind. Your tricks

seven, eight
come centuries too late

nine, ten
for experienced men

eleven, twelve
like myself

thirteen, fourteen
so just be careful to be more seen

fifteen, sixteen
than heard, or preferably not seen

seventeen, eighteen
at all. Or you could stop baiting

nineteen, twenty
and pity me.

John Mole

Until I Saw the Sea

Until I saw the sea
I did not know
that wind
could wrinkle water so.

I never knew
that sun
could splinter a whole sea of blue.

Nor
did I know before
a sea breathes in and out
upon a shore.

Lilian Moore

Western isle

I dream of a western isle
where urchins smile;
where bamboos sigh
and palm trees brush the edges of the sky;
where clouds are feathery plumes
or scrubbed-white furry spumes
or mounds of thunderous black;
where rain comes smart and heavy, with a smack
of bright blue lightning
(splendid – not frightening);
where the sky drowns in the sea's blue;
where in the mornings, mountains steal a deeper hue
from the blue sea and mist it in;
where birds and bees win
honey from eternal flowers;
where trees are limp with bearing
and all taking is sharing;
where air is pure, where men and beast step sure,
where no one counts the hours as they pass –
where every made thing praises
and amazes.

Pamela Mordecai

Winter Morning

Winter is the king of showmen,
Turning tree stumps into snow men
And houses into birthday cakes
And spreading sugar over lakes.
Smooth and clean and frosty white,
The world looks good enough to bite.
That's the season to be young,
Catching snow flakes on your tongue.

Snow is snowy when it's snowing,
I'm sorry it's slushy when it's going.

Ogden Nash

Lord Neptune

Build me a castle,
the young boy cried,
as he tapped his father's knee.
But make it tall
and make it wide,
with a king's throne just for me.

An echo drifted on the wind,
sang deep and wild and free:
Oh you can be king of the castle,
but I am lord of the sea.

Give me your spade,
the father cried;
let's see what we can do!
We'll make it wide
so it holds the tide,
with a fine throne just for you.

He dug deep down
in the firm damp sand,
for the tide was falling fast.
The moat was deep,
the ramparts high,
and the turrets tall and vast.

Now I am king,
the young boy cried,
and this is my golden throne!
I rule the sands,
I rule the seas;
I'm lord of all lands, alone!

The sand-king ruled
from his golden court
and it seemed the wind had died;
but at dusk his throne
sank gently down
in Neptune's rolling tide.

And an echo rose upon the wind,
sang deep and wild and free:
Oh you may be king of the castle,
but I am lord of the sea.

Judith Nicholls

Give Yourself a Hug

Give yourself a hug
when you feel unloved

Give yourself a hug
when people put on airs
to make you feel a bug

Give yourself a hug
when everyone seems to give you
a cold-shoulder shrug

Give yourself a hug –
a big big hug

And keep on singing,
'Only one in a million like me
Only one in a million-billion-thrillion-zillion
like me.'

Grace Nichols

What is Orange?

Orange is a tiger lily,
A carrot,
A feather from
A parrot,
A flame,
The wildest color
You can name.
Orange is a happy day
Saying good-by
In a sunset that
Shocks the sky.
Orange is brave
Orange is bold
It's bittersweet
And marigold.
Orange is zip
Orange is dash
The brightest stripe
In a Roman sash.
Orange is an orange
Also a mango
Orange is music
Of the tango.

Orange is the fur
Of the fiery fox,
The brightest crayon
In the box.
And in the fall
When the leaves are turning
Orange is the smell
Of a bonfire burning....

Mary O'Neill

Dawn Wail for the Dead

Dim light of daybreak now
Faintly over the sleeping camp.
Old lubra first to wake remembers:
First thing every dawn
Remember the dead, cry for them.
Softly at first her wail begins,
One by one as they wake and hear,
Join in the cry, and the whole camp
Wails for the dead, the poor dead
Gone from here to the Dark Place:
They are remembered.
Then it is over, life now,
Fires lit, laughter now,
And a new day calling.

Oodgeroo of the tribe Noonuccal
(formerly known as Kath Walker)

The World the First Time

What is that howling, my mother
Howling out of the sky;
What is it rustles the branches and leaves
And throws the cold snow in my eye?

That is the wind, my wolf son,
The breath of the world passing by,
That flattens the grasses and whips up the lake
And hurls clouds and birds through the sky.

What is that eye gleaming red, mother
Gleaming red in the face of the sky;
Why does it stare at me so mother
Why does its fire burn my eye?

That is the sun, my wolf child,
That changes dark night into day,
That warms your fur and the pine-needled floor
And melts the cold snows away.

And who is this serpent that glides, mother,
And winds the dark rocks among,
And laughs and sings as he glides through my paws
And feels so cool on my tongue?

That is the river, my curious son,
That no creature alive can outrun
He cuts out the valleys and watery lakes
And was here when the world first begun.

And whose is that face that I see, mother,
That face in the water so clear,
Why when I try to catch him
Does he suddenly disappear?

He is closer to you than your brother,
Closer than your father or me,
He'll run beside you your long life through,
For it is yourself – that you see.

Gareth Owen

Mulga Bill's Bicycle

'Twas Mulga Bill, from Eaglehawk, that caught the
    cycling craze;
He turned away the good old horse that served him
    many days;
He dressed himself in cycling clothes, resplendent to
    be seen;
He hurried off to town and bought a shining new machine;
And as he wheeled it through the door, with air of
    lordly pride,
The grinning shop assistant said, 'Excuse me, can you
    ride?'

'See here, young man,' said Mulga Bill, 'from Walgett to
   the sea,
From Conroy's Gap to Castlereagh, there's none can ride
   like me.
I'm good all round at everything, as everybody knows,
Although I'm not the one to talk – I hate a man that blows.'

'But riding is my special gift, my chiefest, sole delight;
Just ask a wild duck can it swim, a wild cat can it fight.
There's nothing clothed in hair or hide, or built of flesh or
   steel,
There's nothing walks or jumps, or runs, on axle, hoof or
   wheel,
But what I'll sit, while hide will hold and girths and straps
   are tight;
I'll ride this here two-wheeled concern right straight away
   at sight.'

'Twas Mulga Bill, from Eaglehawk, that sought his own
   abode,
That perched above the Dead Man's Creek, beside the
   mountain road.
He turned the cycle down the hill and mounted for the fray,
But ere he'd gone a dozen yards it bolted clean away.
It left the track, and through the trees, just like a silver streak,
It whistled down the awful slope towards the Dead Man's
   Creek.

It shaved a stump by half an inch, it dodged a big
    white-box;
The very wallaroos in fright went scrambling up the rocks,
The wombats hiding in their caves dug deeper
    underground,
But Mulga Bill, as white as chalk, sat tight to every bound.
It struck a stone and gave a spring that cleared a fallen tree,
It raced beside a precipice as close as close could be;
And then, as Mulga Bill let out one last despairing shriek,
It made a leap of twenty feet into the Dead Man's Creek.

'Twas Mulga Bill, from Eaglehawk, that slowly swam
    ashore:
He said, 'I've had some narrer shaves and lively rides
    before;
I've rode a wild bull round a yard to win a five-pound
    bet,
But this was sure the derndest ride that I've encountered
    yet.
I'll give that two-wheeled outlaw best; it's shaken all my
    nerve
To feel it whistle through the air and plunge and buck
    and swerve.
It's safe at rest in Dead Man's Creek – we'll leave it lying
    still:
A horse's back is good enough henceforth for Mulga
    Bill.'

A.B. (Banjo) Paterson

The Newcomer

'There's something new in the river,'
The fish said as it swam.
'It's got no scales, no fins, no gills,
And ignores the impassable dam.'

'There's something new in the trees,'
I heard a bloated thrush sing,
'It's got no beak, no claws, no feathers,
And not even the ghost of a wing.'

'There's something new in the warren,'
The rabbit said to the doe,
'It's got no fur, no eyes, no paws,
Yet digs deeper than we can go.'

'There's something new in the whiteness,'
Said the snow-bright polar bear,
'I saw it's shadow on the glacier
But it left no foot-prints there.'

Throughout the animal kingdom
The news was spreading fast –

No beak no claws no feathers,
No scales no fur no gills,
It lives in the trees and the water,
In the earth and the snow and the hills,
And it kills and it kills and it kills.

Brian Patten

It Makes a Change

There's nothing makes a Greenland Whale
Feel half so high-and-mighty,
As sitting on a mantelpiece
In Aunty Mabel's nighty.

It makes a change from Freezing Seas,
(Of which a Whale can tire),
To warm his weary tail at ease
Before an English fire.

For this delight he leaves the sea,
(Unknown to Aunty Mabel),
Returning only when the dawn
Lights up the breakfast table.

Mervyn Peake

What Happens to the Colors?

What happens to the colors
when night replaces day?
What turns the wrens to ravens,
the trees to shades of gray?

Who paints away the garden
when the sky's a sea of ink?
Who robs the sleeping flowers
of their purple and their pink?

What makes the midnight clover
quiver black upon the lawn?
What happens to the colors?
What brings them back at dawn?

Jack Prelutsky

The Bogus-Boo

The Bogus-boo
Is a creature who
Comes out at night—and why?
He likes the air;
He likes to scare
The nervous passer-by.

Out from the park
At dead of dark
He comes with huffling pad.
If, when alone,
You hear his moan,
'Tis like to drive you mad.

He has two wings,
Pathetic things,
With which he cannot fly.
His tusks look fierce,
Yet could not pierce
The merest butterfly.

He has six ears,
But what he hears
Is very faint and small;
And with the claws
On his eight paws
He cannot scratch at all.

He looks so wise
With his owl-eyes,
His aspect grim and ghoulish;
But truth to tell,
He sees not well
And is distinctly foolish.

This Bogus-boo,
What can he do
But huffle in the dark?
So don't take fright;
He has no bite
And very little bark.

James Reeves

Eletelephony

Once there was an elephant,
Who tried to use the telephant—
No! no! I mean an elephone
Who tried to use the telephone—
(Dear me! I am not certain quite
That even now I've got it right.)

Howe'er it was, he got his trunk
Entangled in the telephunk;
The more he tried to get it free,
The louder buzzed the telephee—
(I fear I'd better drop the song
Of elephop and telephong!)

Laura E. Richards

The Paint Box

'Cobalt and umber and ultramarine,
Ivory black and emerald green—
What shall I paint to give pleasure to you?'
'Paint for me somebody utterly new.'

'I have painted you tigers in crimson and white.'
'The colors were good and you painted aright.'
'I have painted the cook and a camel in blue
And a panther in purple.' 'You painted them true.'

'Now mix me a color that nobody knows,
And paint me a country where nobody goes.
And put in it people a little like you,
Watching a unicorn drinking the dew.'

E. V. Rieu

Grammar

The teacher said:
A noun is a naming word.
What is the naming word in the sentence:
'He named the ship *Lusitania*'?
'Named,' said George.
Wrong, it's 'ship'.
Oh, said George.

The teacher said:
A verb is a doing word.
What is the doing word in the sentence:
'I like doing homework'?
'Doing,' said George.
Wrong, it's 'like'.
Oh, said George.

The teacher said:
An adjective is a describing word.
What is the describing word in the sentence:
'Describing sunsets is boring'?
'Describing,' said George.
Wrong, it's 'boring'.
I know it is, said George.

Michael Rosen

Fog

The fog comes
on little cat feet.

It sits looking
over harbour and city
on silent haunches
and then moves on.

Carl Sandburg

Grannie

I stayed with her when I was six then went
To live elsewhere when I was eight years old.
For ages I remembered her faint scent
Of lavender, the way she'd never scold
No matter what I'd done, and most of all
The way her smile seemed, somehow, to enfold
My whole world like a warm, protective shawl.

I knew that I was safe when she was near,
She was so tall, so wide, so large, she would
Stand mountainous between me and my fear,
Yet oh, so gentle, and she understood
Every hope and dream I ever had.
She praised me lavishly when I was good,
But never punished me when I was bad.

Years later war broke out and I became
A soldier and was wounded while in France.
Back home in hospital, still very lame,
I realized suddenly that circumstance
Had brought me close to that small town where she
Was living still. And so I seized the chance
To write and ask if she could visit me.

She came. And I still vividly recall
The shock that I received when she appeared
That dark cold day. Huge grannie was so small!
A tiny, frail, old lady. It was weird.
She hobbled through the ward to where I lay
And drew quite close and, hesitating, peered.
And then she smiled: and love lit up the day.

Vernon Scannell

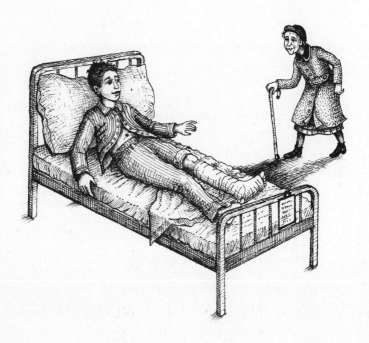

Anne and the Fieldmouse

We found a mouse in the chalk quarry today
In a circle of stones and empty oil drums
By the fag end of a fire. There had been
A picnic there: he must have been after the crumbs.

Jane saw him first, a flicker of brown fur
In and out of the charred wood and chalk-white.
I saw him last, but not till we'd turned up
Every stone and surprised him into flight.

Though not far – little zigzags spurts from stone
To stone. Once, as he lurked in his hiding-place,
I saw his beady eyes uplifted to mine.
I'd never seen such terror in so small a face.

I watched, amazed and guilty. Beside us suddenly
A heavy pheasant whirred up from the ground,
Scaring us all: and, before we knew it, the mouse
Had broken cover, skimming away without a sound,

Melting into the nettles. We didn't go
Till I'd chalked in capitals on a rusty can:
THERE'S A MOUSE IN THOSE NETTLES. LEAVE
HIM ALONE. NOVEMBER 15TH. ANNE.

Ian Serraillier

121

The Little Boy and the Old Man

Said the little boy, 'Sometimes I drop my spoon.'
Said the little old man, 'I do that too.'
The little boy whispered, 'I wet my pants.'
'I do that too,' laughed the little old man.
Said the little boy, 'I often cry.'
The old man nodded, 'So do I.'
'But worst of all,' said the boy, 'it seems
Grown-ups don't pay attention to me.'
And he felt the warmth of a wrinkled old hand.
'I know what you mean,' said the little old man.

Shel Silverstein

Hallowe'en

At night we walked the street.
I was wearing my wolf face.

The moon was shining brightly
and I began to howl.

The moon was like a plate.
I howled like a hungry wolf.

I howled and howled and howled,
till I met the lion.

Mask to mask we stood,
and our hair bristled.

Iain Crichton Smith

Seal

See how he dives
From the rocks with a zoom!
See how he darts
Through his watery room
Past crabs and eels
And green seaweed,
Past fluffs of sandy
Minnow feed!
See how he swims
With a swerve and a twist,
A flip of the flipper,
A flick of the wrist!
Quicksilver-quick,
Softer than spray,
Down he plunges

Before you can think,
Before you can utter
Words like 'Dill pickle'
Or 'Apple butter',
Back up he swims
Past Sting Ray and Shark,
Out with a zoom,
A whoop, a bark;
Before you can say
Whatever you wish,
He plops at your side
With a mouthful of fish!

William Jay Smith

Flowers Are a Silly Bunch

Flowers are a silly bunch
While trees are sort of bossy.
Lakes are shy
The earth is calm
And rivers do seem saucy.
Hills are good
But mountains mean
While weeds all ask for pity.
I guess the country can be nice
But I prefer the city.

Arnold Spilka

The Shell

And then I pressed the shell
    Close to my ear
And listened well,
And straightway like a bell
    Came low and clear
The slow, sad murmur of far distant seas,
Whipped by an icy breeze
    Upon a shore
Windswept and desolate,

It was a sunless strand that never bore
The footprint of a man,
     Nor felt the weight
Since time began
Of any human quality or stir
Save what the dreary winds and waves incur.
And in the hush of waters was the sound
Of pebbles rolling round,
For ever rolling with a hollow sound.
And bubbling sea-weeds as the waters go
Swish to and fro
Their long, cold tentacles of slimy grey.
There was no day,
Nor ever came a night
Setting the stars alight
To wonder at the moon:
Was twilight only and the frightened croon,
Smitten to whimpers, of the dreary wind
And waves that journeyed blind –
And then I loosed my ear – oh, it was sweet
To hear a cart go jolting down the street!

James Stephens

The Mewlips

The shadows where the Mewlips dwell
Are dark and wet as ink,
And slow and softly rings their bell,
As in the slime you sink.

You sink into the slime, who dare
To knock upon their door,
While down the grinning gargoyles stare
And noisome waters pour.

Beside the rotting river-strand
The drooping willows weep,
And gloomily the gorcrows stand
Croaking in their sleep.

Over the Merlock Mountains a long and weary way,
In a mouldy valley where the trees are grey,
By a dark pool's borders without wind or tide,
Moonless and sunless, the Mewlips hide.

The cellars where the Mewlips sit
Are deep and dank and cold
With single sickly candle lit;
And there they count their gold.

Their walls are wet, their ceilings drip;
　　Their feet upon the floor
Go softly with a squish–flap–flip,
　　As they sidle to the door.

They peep out slyly; through a crack
　　Their feeling fingers creep,
And when they've finished, in a sack
　　Your bones they take to keep.

Beyond the Merlock Mountains, a long and lonely road,
Through the spider-shadows and the marsh of Tode,
And through the wood of hanging trees and the
　　gallows-weed,
You go to find the Mewlips – and the Mewlips feed.

J.R.R. Tolkien

The Swing

The garden-swing at the lawn's edge
Is hung beneath the hawthorn-hedge;
White branches droop above, and shed
Their petals on the swinger's head.
Here, now the day is almost done,
And leaves are pierced by the last sun,
I sit where hawthorn-breezes creep
Round me, and swing the hours to sleep:
Swinging alone –
By myself alone –
Alone,
Alone,
Alone.

In a soft shower the hawthorn-flakes descend.
Dusk falls at last. The dark-leaved branches bend
Earthward... The longest dream must have an end.

    Now in my bedroom half-undressed,
    My face against the window pressed,
    I see once more the things which day
    Gave me, and darkness takes away:
    The garden-path still dimly white,
    The lawn, the flower-beds sunk in night,
    And, brushed by some uncertain breeze,
    A ghostly swing beneath ghostly trees:
    Swinging alone –
    By itself alone –
    Alone,
    Alone,
    Alone.

John Walsh

Magic Story of Falling Asleep

When the last giant came out of his cave
and his bones turned into the mountain
and his clothes turned into the flowers,

nothing was left but his tooth
which my dad took home in his truck
which my granddad carved into a bed

which my mum tucks me into at night
when I dream of the last giant
when I fall asleep on the mountain.

Nancy Willard

The Traveller

Old man, old man, sitting on the stile,
Your boots are worn, your clothes are torn,
  Tell us why you smile.

Children, children, what silly things you are!
My boots are worn and my clothes are torn
  Because I've walked so far.

Old man, old man, where have you walked from?
Your legs are bent, your breath is spent –
  Which way did you come?

Children, children, when you're old and lame,
When your legs are bent and your breath is spent
  You'll know the way I came.

Old man, old man, have you far to go
Without a friend to your journey's end,
  And why are you so slow?

Children, children, I do the best I may:
I meet with a friend at my journey's end
  With whom you'll meet some day.

Old man, old man, sitting on the stile,
How do you know which way to go,
   And why is it you smile?

Children, children, butter should be spread,
Floors should be swept and promises kept –
   And you should be in bed!

Raymond Wilson

pumpkin

After its lid
Is cut, the slick
Seeds and stuck
Wet strings
Scooped out,
Walls scraped
Dry and white,
Face carved, candle
Fixed and lit,

Light creeps
Into the thick
Rind: giving
That dead orange
Vegetable skull
Warm skin, making
A live head
To hold its
Sharp gold grin.

Valerie Worth

Rainforest

The forest drips and glows with green.
The tree-frog croaks his far-off song.
His voice is stillness, moss and rain
drunk from the forest ages long.

We cannot understand that call
unless we move into his dream,
where all is one and one is all
and frog and python are the same.

We with our quick dividing eyes
measure, distinguish and are gone.
The forest burns, the tree-frog dies,
yet one is all and all are one.

Judith Wright

What Was It?

What was it
that could make
me wake
in the middle of the night
when the light
was a long way from coming
and the humming
of the fridge was the single
tingle
of sound
all round?

Why, when I crept downstairs and watched
green numbers sprinting on the kitchen clock,
was I afraid the empty rocking chair
might start to rock?

Why, when I stole back up and heard
the creak of each stair to my own
heart's quickening beats,

was I afraid that I should find
some other thing from the night outside
between my sheets?

Kit Wright

Dragon Night

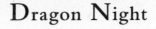

Little flame mouths,
Cool your tongues.
Dreamtime starts,
My furnace lungs.

Rest your wings now,
Little flappers,
Cave mouth calls
To dragon nappers.

Night is coming,
Bank your fire.
Time for dragons
To retire.

Hiss.
Hush.
Sleep.

Jane Yolen

I Love Me Mudder...

I love me mudder and me mudder love me
we come so far from over de sea,
we heard dat de streets were paved with gold
sometime it hot sometime it cold
I love me mudder and me mudder love me
we try fe live in harmony
you might know her as Valerie
but to me she is my mummy.

She shouts at me daddy so loud some time
she don't smoke weed she don't drink wine
she always do the best she can
she work damn hard down ina England,
she's always singing some kind of song
she have big muscles and she very very strong
she likes pussy cats and she love cashew nuts
she don't bother with no if and buts.

I love me mudder and me mudder love me
we come so far from over de sea
we heard dat de streets were paved with gold
sometime it hot sometime it cold,
I love her and she love me too
and dis is a love I know is true
me an my mudder we love you too.

Benjamin Zephaniah

So Will I

My grandfather remembers long ago
the white Queen Anne's lace that grew wild.
He remembers the buttercups and goldenrod
from when he was a child.

He remembers long ago
the white snow falling falling,
He remembers the bluebird and thrush
at twilight
calling, calling.

He remembers long ago
The new moon in the summer sky
He remembers the wind in the trees
and its long, rising sigh.
And so will I
        so will I.

Charlotte Zolotow

Index of Titles and First Lines

— Biographical Notes —

JOHN AGARD (b.1949) is a British Afro-Caribbean poet who was born in Guyana and has lived in Britain since 1977. He has edited collections for children, such as *Why is the Sky?* and for teenagers – *Life Doesn't Frighten Me At All.* He has performed his poems in over 2000 schools in the UK; his own collections for children include *I Din Do Nuttin, Laughter Is An Egg* and *We Animals Would Like a Word With You.* John Agard has also written plays for children.

ALLAN AHLBERG (b.1938) trained to be a teacher, but was a plumber's mate and gravedigger before spending ten years teaching. After teaching he became a full-time writer of children's books, many of which have been best-sellers, such as *The Jolly Postman,* illustrated by his wife Janet. His poetry books include the immensely popular *Please Mrs Butler* and *Heard It In The Playground.*

DOROTHY ALDIS (1896-1966) was born in Chicago, USA where her father worked as a newspaper editor. She wrote many stories and poems for children. Her poetry books include *All Together, Here, There and Everywhere* and *Is Anybody Hungry?*

GEORGE BARKER (1913-1991) grew up in a block of tenement flats in Chelsea. His first book of poems was published when was twenty-two. He once said, "If I didn't write poetry, I would explode." His poetry for children includes *Runes and Rhymes and Tunes and Chimes, To Aylsham Fair* and *The Alphabetical Zoo.*

HILAIRE BELLOC (1870-1953) was born in France to Anglo-French parents, brought up in England and went to Oxford University. He became a British subject and was elected to Parliament, serving two terms as an M.P. During his lifetime he was renowned for his novels and adult writing, but today he is best known for his children's poetry, in particular for his cautionary verses.

GERARD BENSON (b.1931) is an anthologist and poet, who in 1991 won the Signal Poetry Award for his anthology *This Poem Doesn't Rhyme.* He was one of the people responsible for starting the project Poems on the Underground which introduced poems among the advertisements in London Underground carriages. His own collections for young people include *The Magnificent Callisto.*

JAMES BERRY (b.1924) was born in Jamaica, but has lived in Britain since 1948. He is an acclaimed adult poet who won the Poetry Society's National Competition in 1981 and has edited various anthologies of poetry. His own collection of poems for young people, *When I Dance,* which draws on experiences from the inner-city life of Britain and from the rural Caribbean, won the Signal Poetry Award. He has also won the Smarties Prize for Children's Books for his collection of short stories *A Thief in the Village.*

VALERIE BLOOM (b.1956) grew up in a large family, the second of nine brothers and sisters, in a small village in Jamaica. She worked as a librarian before training as a teacher. She studied at the University of Kent, before becoming a Multicultural Arts Officer in Manchester. She now concentrates on writing and performing her poems in schools and libraries. Her collections include *Let Me Touch the Sky* and *The World Is Sweet.*

GWENDOLYN BROOKS (b.1917) is an African-American writer, who in 1950 won the Pulitzer Prize for her book of poems, *Annie Allen* and was chosen as Poet Laureate for the state of Illinois. She is also the author of a picture book for children, *The Tiger Who Wore White Gloves.*

MARGARET WISE BROWN (1910-1952) was born in New York, USA. She wrote many stories for children, some of them under the pseudonym Golden Macdonald. She published several collections of poetry, including *The Dark Wood of the Golden Birds* and *Nibble Nibble.*

CHARLES CAUSLEY (b.1917) was born in Launceston in Cornwall. As a young man he worked in various offices and played in a dance band. After serving in the Royal Navy during the Second World War, he trained as a teacher. He began writing, but was in his fifties before he became a full-time writer. He has won many prizes including the Signal Poetry Award. His collections of poetry for children include *Figgie Hobbin* and *All Day Saturday*.

JOHN CIARDI (1916-1986) was born in Boston, USA. He had a distinguished literary career and wrote poems for adults and children. His books for children include *The Monster Den* and *You Know Who*.

LEONARD CLARK (1905-1981) was born in Guernsey, but was brought up by a foster-mother in a small mining town in the Forest of Dean. He worked as a teacher and then as an Inspector of Schools. He published numerous books, editing anthologies as well as writing collections of his own poems for children such as *Secret As Toads* and *The Singing Time*.

ELIZABETH COATSWORTH (1893-1986) was born in Buffalo, New York, USA. As a child she travelled extensively, visiting Europe, north Africa and Mexico. She wrote stories and poems for adults and children. Her poetry books for children include *Night and the Cat*.

FRANK COLLYMORE (1893-1980) was born in the West Indian island of Barbados and grew up to become one of his country's leading literary figures. He was a teacher and editor of a literary magazine BIM and wrote short stories and plays as well as several collections of poetry. In 1958 he was awarded an O.B.E.

STANLEY COOK (1922-1991) was born and brought up in a Yorkshire village and educated at Doncaster Grammar School and Oxford University. He taught in schools in Lancashire and Yorkshire before becoming a lecturer at Huddersfield Polytechnic. As well as volumes of children's verse such as *The Dragon on the Wall* and *The Squirrel in Town* he also published a book of concrete poetry.

WENDY COPE (b.1945) was born in Kent and studied history at Oxford University. She worked as a primary teacher before becoming a full-time writer. She says: "It was partly as a result of encouraging children to read and write poetry in the classroom that I began to try it myself." As well as collections of her own poems, such as *Making Cocoa For Kingsley Amis* she has edited a number of anthologies, including *Is That the New Moon?*, a collection of poems by women poets.

ROALD DAHL (1916-1990) was born in Llandaff in Wales. After leaving school, he joined the Shell Oil Company, then served in the RAF as a fighter pilot, before being transferred into Intelligence and ending the war as a Wing Commander. After the war he became a writer. He is one of todays most popular children's writers and several of his books, including *Charlie and the Chocolate Factory* and *Matilda* have been made into successful films. Many of his adult short stories were dramatised for television in the series *Tales of the Unexpected*.

WALTER DE LA MARE (1873-1956) was born in Kent and as a young man worked as a book-keeper. His first book was published under the name Walter Ramal, which is part of his surname read backwards. He became famous following the publication of *The Listeners and Other Poems*. In addition to collections of his own poetry, he also edited a number of anthologies such as *Come Hither*.

BERLIE DOHERTY (b.1943) writes picture books, poetry, plays and novels for children. She won the Carnegie Medal for her novel for young adults, *Dear Nobody*. Her poetry for children includes the collection *Walking On Air*.

CAROL ANN DUFFY (b.1955) is renowned for her poetry for adults. Her anthology of poems about death and loss, *Stopping for Death*, won the Signal Poetry Award. She has published two collections for children, *Meeting Midnight* and *The Oldest Girl in the World*.

MICHAEL DUGAN (b.1947) was born in Melbourne, Australia and is well-known in his native country for his books of humorous verse for children, such as *Unbalanced Poems* and *Flocks' Socks and Other Shocks*. He has also edited a number of poetry anthologies, including *Stuff and Nonsense*.

RICHARD EDWARDS (b.1949) was born in Kent and educated at Sevenoaks School and the University of Warwick. He is a part-time teacher who has lived in Italy, France and Spain. He has written several collections of children's poems, including *The Word Party*, *Leopards on Mars* and *Teaching the Parrot*.

T. S. ELIOT (1886-1965) was born in St Louis, USA but lived in England from 1914. He was a distinguished adult poet who was awarded the Nobel Prize for Literature in 1948. His many books include *Old Possum's Book of Practical Cats*, on which the hit musical *Cats* was based.

GAVIN EWART (b.1916) served in the Second World War and later worked for the British Council and as an advertising copywriter. He is most well-known for his poetry for adults. His children's poems include the collection *The Learned Hippopotamus: Poems Conveying Useful Information About Animals Ordinary and Extraordinary*.

ELEANOR FARJEON (1881-1965) wrote her first poem when she was six. She never went to school, but was taught at home by a governess. She was encouraged to write by her father, who was himself a writer. She published over 80 books and won many prizes for her writing. Her books include *The Little Bookroom* and *Kings and Queens*, which she wrote in collaboration with her brother Herbert, and *Blackbird Has Spoken*, a selection of her children's poems.

MAX FATCHEN (b.1920) grew up on a farm near Adelaide in Australia. He became a journalist and travelled extensively, writing about dozens of major events and disasters. He likes the sea and fishing and is a keen cricket fan. His books of poetry for children include *Songs For My Dog and Other People*, *Peculiar Rhymes and Lunatic Lines* and *A Paddock of Poems*.

RACHEL FIELD (1894-1942) was born in New York. She wrote adult novels, one of which was made into a successful film, but she is best known for her children's stories and poems. Her poetry collections for children include *Taxis and Toadstools*.

AILEEN FISHER (b.1906) grew up on a farm in Michigan, USA. She loves the country, and once said, "My day is not complete unless I have a good walk on a mountain trail with the dogs." In 1978 she received the Excellence in Poetry for Children Award presented by the National Council of Teachers of English.

ROY FULLER (1912-1991) was a distinguished adult poet who was awarded the Queen's Medal for Poetry. He began writing children's poetry for his grandchildren. His books include a volume of his collected verse for children – *The World Through the Window*.

ROSE FYLEMAN (1877-1957) was born in Nottingham. After working as a teacher for a few years, she studied singing in Germany and Paris. She wrote plays, stories and poems for children and was a regular contributor to *Punch* magazine.

NIKKI GIOVANNI (b.1943) is an African-American writer who was born in Tennessee, USA. Her collections of poetry, such as *Spin a Soft Black Song* capture the experience of young African Americans.

GRACE WALKER GORDON is a Jamaican writer and teacher who has taught at the University of the West Indies. She has worked extensively in children's theatre and written many textbooks as well as poetry.

HARRY GRAHAM (1874-1936) was born in London and served as a captain in the Coldstream Guards. He is chiefly known for rhymes from two of his collections – *Ruthless Rhymes for Heartless Homes* and *More Ruthless Rhymes for Heartless Homes*.

Kenneth Grahame (1859-1932) is famous as the author of *The Wind in the Willows*. He was born in Edinburgh, but went to school in Oxford. After school he went to work at the Bank of England. *The Wind in the Willows* began as a series of bedtime stories, which he told to his son.

Robert Graves (1895-1985) was born in London and served in the army in the First World War. After the war, he wrote an account of his experiences in *Good-Bye to All That*. Its success enabled him to emigrate to Majorca in 1929. He wrote many books for adults, including historical novels such as *I, Claudius*. His collections of poetry for children include *The Penny Fiddle*.

Philip Gross (b.1952) was born in Cornwall, the son of a Displaced Person from Estonia and a Cornish mother. He was educated at Sussex University and worked in publishing and in libraries before becoming a full-time writer. His books for children include novels such as *The Wind Gate* and poetry collections such as *Manifold Manor* and *The All-Nite Café*.

Thomas Hardy (1840-1928) is famous as the author of *Tess of the D'Urbervilles* and *Far From the Madding Crowd*, set in the countryside around Dorset, where he spent most of his life. Before becoming a writer, he trained as an architect. He published eight volumes of poetry.

Seamus Heaney (b.1939) is internationally renowned for his adult poetry. He lives in Dublin, but was born in County Derry, Northern Ireland. He was elected Professor of Poetry at Oxford University in 1989. Together with Ted Hughes he edited two collections designed to introduce young people to the world of poetry – *The Rattle Bag* and *The School Bag*.

Adrian Henri (1932-2000) was born in Birkenhead and was one of the group known as the Liverpool Poets in the 1960s. He was a painter and musician as well as a poet. His collections for children include *The Phantom Lollipop Lady* and *The World's Your Lobster*.

Phoebe Hesketh (b.1909) was born in Preston, Lancashire and educated at Cheltenham Ladies College. She was a freelance journalist and a college lecturer and has won prizes for her poetry for adults.

Russell Hoban (b.1925) was born in Pennsylvania, USA but has lived in England since 1969. He went to art school before serving in the Second World War, then worked as a freelance illustrator for eight years before becoming a full-time writer. As well as his poetry collections, such as *The Pedalling Man* and *The Last of the Wallendas*, he is the author of several picture books, including the award winning *How Tom Beat Captain Najork and the Hired Sportsmen,* and the ever popular storybook *The Mouse and His Child*.

Mary Ann Hoberman (b.1930) was born in Connecticut, USA. She has written many poetry books for children, a large number of which have been illustrated by her husband, Norman Hoberman, an architect.

Langston Hughes (1902-1967) was among the foremost of African-American writers. He was extremely prolific, writing novels, short stories, plays, newspaper columns and children's books, in addition to his many volumes of poetry.

Ted Hughes (1930-1998) was born in Yorkshire. A distinguished adult poet, he was appointed Poet Laureate in 1984. He wrote many books for children including stories such as *How the Whale Became* and *The Iron Man*. His books of poetry for children includes *Season Songs* and *Meet My Folks*.

Elizabeth Jennings (b.1926) was born in Lincolnshire and has lived in Oxford for most of her life. She has won many awards for her poetry for adults. Among her books for children is *A Spell of Words: Selected poems for children*.

JENNY JOSEPH (b.1932) was born in Birmingham. She has worked as a journalist, an adult education lecturer and a pub landlady. She is the author of one of the nation's favourite poems *Warning* and her collections for children include *All the Things I See*.

JACKIE KAY (b.1961) grew up in Glasgow and had her first poem published at the age of twelve in the *Morning Star*. She studied English at Stirling University, then moved to London and had various jobs including working at a Children's Centre and as a hospital porter. She has written for theatre, television and radio and is a novelist as well as a poet. Her first collection for children, *Two's Company* won the 1993 Signal Poetry Award. Her other collections include *Three Has Gone* and *The Frog Who Dreamed She Was an Opera Singer*.

X. J. KENNEDY (b.1929) was born in New Jersey, USA. He served in the US Navy and was a university teacher before becoming a full-time writer. He has written textbooks and a children's novel as well as books of children's poems.

RUDYARD KIPLING (1865-1936) was born in Bombay, India. His parents were English and from 1899 onwards he lived mainly in England. He is most well-known for his classic stories, *The Jungle Book* and the *Just So Stories*. In 1907 he was awarded the Nobel Prize for Literature.

JAMES KIRKUP (b.1923) grew up in South Shields where his father was a joiner. He is fluent in several languages, has published translations of French and Japanese books, and taught English in universities in Japan. He is renowned for his poetry for both adults and children and has written plays and an account of his childhood, *The Only Child*.

KARLA KUSKIN (b.1932) was born in Manhattan, New York, USA. She studied graphic design at college, and had various jobs, including working for a fashion photographer and an advertising agency, before becoming a full-time writer and illustrator. In 1979 she received the Award for Excellence in Poetry for Children presented by the National Council of Teachers for English.

BRIAN LEE (b.1935) was born in Ealing, west London and grew up during the Second World War. He worked as a journalist, before taking an English degree and becoming a teacher. His books of poetry for children include *Late Home*.

DENNIS LEE (b.1939) was born in Toronto, Canada. For four years he worked as a songwriter for the television programme *Fraggle Rock*. His popular books of poetry for children include *Alligator Pie* and *Jelly Belly*.

MYRA COHN LIVINGSTON (b.1926) was born in Nebraska, USA. After college, she worked for some years as a professional French horn player. She has written many books of poems for children, such as *Monkey Puzzle and other poems* and edited numerous anthologies. In 1980 she received the Award for Excellence in Poetry for Children presented by the National Council of Teachers of English.

CHRISTOPHER LOGUE (b.1926) was born in Portsmouth and went to Portsmouth Grammar School. He has written plays and screenplays and been a regular contributor to *Private Eye* magazine, as well as being an actor and poetry-performer. He has edited a number of anthologies for children including *The Children's Book of Children's Rhymes*.

EDWARD LOWBURY (b.1913) was born in London and studied medicine at Oxford University. He became a distinguished research microbiologist, publishing more than 200 research papers and two books on the control of infection. He has also published over twenty collections of his poetry, including *Green Magic*, a collection of his poems for children.

DAVID McCORD (b.1897) was born in New York, USA. He was an academic, writing books in many fields, including education, art, history and medicine. He wrote several collections of poetry for children, including *Mr Bidery's Spidery Garden*. He received the first National Council of Teachers of English Award for Excellence in Poetry for children.

ROGER MCGOUGH (b. 1937) was born in Liverpool. In the 1960s he was one of the group known as the Liverpool Poets and was a member of a band called *The Scaffold*. He has edited a number of popular anthologies, such as *Strictly Private,* and *One Hundred Best Poems for Children*. His own collections for children include *Sky in the Pie*, *Pillow Talk* and *Bad, Bad Cats*.

MARGARET MAHY (b.1936) was born in New Zealand. She worked as a librarian before becoming a full-time writer. She won the Carnegie Medal for her novel *The Haunting*. Her books of poetry include *The Tin Can Band and other poems*.

JOHN MASEFIELD (1878-1967) joined the Merchant Navy at the age of thirteen. During his second voyage, he left the ship in New York and took a job as a bartender. He then worked in a carpet factory, before returning to England to become a writer. As well as poetry, he wrote plays and novels for children, such as *The Box of Delights*. From 1930 to 1967 he was Poet Laureate.

EVE MERRIAM (b.1916) was born in New York, USA. She has worked as a teacher and in publishing and has produced a number of books for children, including the poetry collections, *There Is No Rhyme for Silver* and *You Be Good & I'll Be Night: Jump-On The Bed Poems*.

SPIKE MILLIGAN (b.1918) was born in India and served in the army during the Second World War. He became famous as a member of the cast of the radio series *The Goon Show* and then as a TV personality. His books of irreverent humorous verse for children include *Silly Verse for Kids, A Book of Milliganimals* and *Startling Verse For All the Family*.

A. A. MILNE (1882-1956) is famous as the author of *Winnie the Pooh* and *The House at Pooh Corner* and his two books of children's verse, *When We Were Very Young* and *Now We Are Six*. These books were written for his son, Christopher Robin. He was also a successful playwright and essayist.

ADRIAN MITCHELL (b.1932) was born in London and educated at Oxford University. He worked as a journalist and has written extensively for both adults and children. Among his books for children are *The Thirteen Secrets of Poetry, Nothingmas Day* and *Balloon Lagoon and the Magic Islands of Poetry*.

JOHN MOLE (b.1941) won the Signal award in 1988 for his collection *Boo to a Goose*. He is also an acclaimed adult poet. He lives in Hertfordshire where he teaches and regularly plays as a jazz clarinettist. His other collections for children include *The Conjuror's Rabbit* and *Hot Air*.

LILIAN MOORE was born in New York, USA. She studied English at college and has worked as a teacher. She specialised in the teaching of reading and has written many stories for beginner readers and edited various reading series.

PAMELA MORDECAI (b.1942)was born in Jamaica and has worked as a teacher. In 1993 her collection *Ezra's Goldfish and Other Story-Poems* won the first Vic Reid Award for Children's Literature in Jamaica. She now lives in Canada.

OGDEN NASH (1902-1971) was born in New York, USA. He worked as a publisher, teacher and journalist and is renowned for his humorous verse. He wrote numerous books, edited collections of stories and wrote lyrics for musical productions. He wrote one book of verse specifically for children – *Parents Keep Out!*

JUDITH NICHOLLS (b.1941) was born in Lincolnshire and went to Skegness Grammar School, before training to be a teacher. She now lives in a cottage in a Wiltshire churchyard and is a full-time writer. She has published over thirty books for children including collections of her own poetry, such as *Magic Mirror* and anthologies, such as *What On Earth…?*

GRACE NICHOLS (b.1950) is a British Afro-Caribbean poet who was born in Guyana, where she worked as a journalist before coming to live in Britain in 1977. Her first book of poems for adults won the Commonwealth Poetry Prize in 1983. Her books of children's poetry include *Come Into My Tropical Garden* and *Give Yourself a Hug*.

MARY O'NEILL was born in New York, USA and educated at Michigan State University. As well as poetry, she has written stories and articles for popular magazines such as *Good Housekeeping* and *Women's Day*. Her collections of poetry for children include *Hailstones and Halibut Bones* and *People I'd Like To Keep*.

OODGEROO OF THE TRIBE NOONUCCAL (b.1920) spent her childhood on Stradbroke Island, off the coast of Queensland, Australia, where her father worked as ganger of an Aboriginal work-force. When she left school, she worked as a domestic help, before serving as a telephonist in the Australian Women's Auxiliary Service and later training as a typist. She was the first Aboriginal poet to have a book of poems published and she has campaigned intensively for Aboriginal rights. In addition to her poems, she has written an autobiographical account of her childhood, *Stradbroke Dreamtime*.

GARETH OWEN (b.1936) was born in Lancashire and says he was "a bit of a failure at school." He left at sixteen and spent three years in the Merchant Navy, then three years doing "dead-end jobs" before training as a teacher. His second book of poems, *Song of the City* won the Signal Poetry Award. As well as poetry, he also writes children's novels, such as *Rosie No-name and the Forest of Forgetting*.

A. B. (BANJO) PATERSON (1864-1941) was born in New South Wales, Australia. He qualified as a solicitor, but then did a variety of jobs, including working as a war correspondent and as a grazier. As a writer, he became known for his bush ballads, the most famous of which are *The Man From Snowy River* and *Waltzing Matilda*.

BRIAN PATTEN (b.1946) was born in Liverpool and in the 1960s was one of the group known as the Liverpool Poets. He is a popular performer of his poetry for both children and adults. His collections for children include *Gargling with Jelly* and *Thawing Frozen Frogs*.

MERVYN PEAKE (1911-1968) was born in China. He is most famous for the trilogy of novels for adults, beginning with *Titus Groan*, which were made into a television series. He was an artist and illustrator of children's books, and his books of poetry for children includes *A Book of Nonsense*.

JACK PRELUTSKY (b.1940) was born in New York, USA. He is well-known both for his many anthologies of children's poetry and his own collections of children's verse. These include *Nightmares and other poems to trouble your sleep* and *The Headless Horseman Rides Tonight – more poems to trouble your sleep*, both illustrated by Arnold Lobel.

JAMES REEVES (1909-1978) was born in London. He is remembered for his children's poetry, although he wrote poetry for adults and also edited and wrote many books about poets and poetry. A volume of his collected poems, *Complete Poems for Children,* was published in 1973.

LAURA E. RICHARDS (1850-1943) was born in Boston, Massachusetts, USA. Her mother was Julia Ward Howe, who wrote "The Battle Hymn of The Republic". She was a prolific writer for adults and children. She began writing at the age of ten, before the outbreak of the American Civil War, and in 1940 wrote a poem about the heroism of the English soldiers at Dunkirk during the Second Word War. Today, she is remembered chiefly for her children's poetry.

E. V. Rieu (1887-1972) was born in London. He worked as a publisher and was the editor of the Penguin Classics series for twenty years, during which time he published a translation of *The Odyssey*. He wrote two books of poetry for children: *Cuckoo Calling: A Book of Verse for Youthful People* and *The Flattered Flying Fish and Other Poems*.

Michael Rosen (b.1946) is one of Britain's foremost children's poets, who has written over a hundred books for children and performed his poems in over a thousand schools. His book *We're Going on a Bear Hunt* won the Smarties Award for Best Book of the Year. He has presented *Poetry Corner* and *Treasure Islands* on BBC radio and in 1997 won the Eleanor Farjeon Award for his contribution to children's literature. His popular collections of poems for children include *Mind Your Own Business*, *Wouldn't You Like To Know* and *Quick, Let's Get Out of Here*.

Carl Sandburg (1878-1967) was born in Illinois, USA. On leaving school he travelled around the Midwestern states, before going as a soldier to Puerto Rico to fight in the Spanish-American War. In addition to writing poetry and prose, he collected and sang folk songs. He won the Pulitzer Prize for his *Complete Poems* and also for his four volume book *The War Years*. His collected poems and stories for children can be found in a book called *The Sandburg Treasury*.

Vernon Scannell (b.1922) was born in Lincolnshire. As a young man he was a boxer before training as a teacher. He writes poetry for both adults and children. His collections for children include *The Apple Raid and Other Poems* and *The Clever Potato*.

Ian Serraillier (1912-1994) is most well-known for his children's novel *The Silver Sword*. Born in London, he worked as a teacher until becoming a full-time writer. His collections of poetry for children include *Thomas and the Sparrow* and *I'll Tell You a Tale*.

Shel Silverstein (1932-1998) was born in Chicago, USA. In addition to being a poet, he was a cartoonist, guitarist, folk-singer, composer and playwright. His books of poems for children, which he illustrated himself, include *Where the Sidewalk Ends* and *A Light in the Attic*, both of which were best-sellers.

Iain Crichton Smith (b.1928) was born on the Scottish island of Lewis and educated in Stornoway and at the University of Aberdeen. He worked as a teacher in Clydebank and Oban before becoming a full-time writer. He won several literary prizes and was awarded an O.B.E. in 1980.

William Jay Smith (b.1918) is an American poet whose poems have appeared in *Cricket* magazine and the *New York Times*. His books of poetry include a collection of his nonsense verse *Laughing Times*.

Arnold Spilka is an American poet. His collections for children include *And the Frog "Blah!"* and *A Lion I Can Do Without*.

James Stephens (1881-1950) was born in Dublin and had no formal education. Nevertheless he became a popular Irish poet, who is also well-known for his humorous story, *The Crock of Gold*.

J. R. R. Tolkien (1892-1973) was an Oxford professor, who is famous as the author of *The Hobbit* and its sequel, the trilogy *The Lord of the Rings*. He wrote his books in a shed at the bottom of his garden.

John Walsh (1911-1972) was born in Brighton and worked as an English teacher. His books of children's poetry include *The Roundabout by the Sea* and *The Truants and other poems for children*.

Nancy Willard (b.1936) was born in Ann Arbor, Michigan, USA. She has written books for adults and children. Her book *A Visit to William Blake's Inn* won the Newbery Award in 1982.

RAYMOND WILSON (1925-1995) was a well-known anthologist of children's verse, as well as being a poet himself. For many years he was Professor of Education at Reading University. His anthologies include *Nine O'Clock Bell: Poems About School* and *Time's Delights*.

VALERIE WORTH (b.1933) was born in Pennsylvania, USA. In 1991 she won the Award for Excellence in Poetry for Children presented by the National Council of Teachers of English. She is renowned for her brief lyrics in her four *Small Poems* books.

JUDITH WRIGHT (b.1915) is a distinguished Australian poet who was born in New South Wales. As well as poetry, she has written stories for children, such as *King of the Dingoes*.

KIT WRIGHT (b.1944) was born in Kent and has worked as a teacher in London and as a university lecturer in Canada. His collections for children include *Rabbiting On*, *Cat Among the Pigeons* and *Great Snakes!*

JANE YOLEN (b.1939) is acclaimed for her picture books, such as *Owl Moon*, as well as her poetry for children. She has also written novels for young adults and received an honorary degree for her writing. Her collections of poetry include *Breakfast, Books and Dreams* and *How Beastly!*

BENJAMIN ZEPHANIAH (b.1958) was born in Birmingham. As a child, he attended a number of different schools, including one in Jamaica, while living with his grandmother. He is a performance poet, who has performed his raps in many places around the world, including Palestine, Argentina and Uruguay. His books of children's poetry include *Talking Turkeys*, *Funky Chickens* and *Wicked World*.

CHARLOTTE ZOLOTOW (b.1915) was born in Norfolk, Virginia, USA and educated at the University of Wisconsin. After college, she took a secretarial job with a publishing company before joining its children's book department, where she became a distinguished editor. She is the author of over 90 books for children.

━ Acknowledgements ━

The publishers gratefully acknowledge the following for permission to reproduce copyright material in this anthology.

John Agard: 'Poetry Jump-Up' from *Get Back Pimple* (Viking, 1996), by permission of John Agard c/o Caroline Sheldon Literary Agency. **Allan Ahlberg**: 'The Old Teacher' from *Heard It In the Playground* (Viking, 1989) copyright © Allan Ahlberg 1989, by permission of Penguin Books Ltd. **Dorothy Aldis**: 'Everybody Says' from *Everything and Anything*, copyright © 1925, 1927, renewed 1953, 1954, 1955 by Dorothy Aldis, by permission of the publishers, G. P. Putnams Sons, an imprint of Penguin Putnam Books for Young Readers, a division of Penguin Putnam Inc. **George Barker**: 'This is a Rune I Have Heard a Tree Say' from *Runes and Rhymes and Tunes and Chimes* (1968), by permission of the publishers, Faber & Faber Ltd. **Hilaire Belloc**: 'Rebecca' from *Cautionary Tales for Children* (Gerald Duckworth), by permission of PFD on behalf of the Estate of Hilaire Belloc. **Gerard Benson**: 'The Hobby Horse' from *The Magnificent Callisto* (Viking, 1992/Smith Doorstop, 2001), by permission of the author. **James Berry**: 'Benediction' from *Chain of Days* (Oxford University Press, 1985), copyright © James Berry 1985, by permission of PFD on behalf of James Berry. **Valerie Bloom**: 'Visit to de Dentist' from *Duppy Jamboree* (Cambridge University Press, 1992), by permission of the author. **Margaret Wise Brown**: 'The Secret Song' from *Nibble, Nibble* (Harper & Row) copyright © 1959 by William Scott, Inc, renewed © 1987 by Roberta Brown Rauch, by permission of HarperCollins*Publishers* (USA). **Charles Causley**: 'Who?' from *Collected Poems* (Macmillan, 1975), by permission of David Higham Associates. **John Ciardi**: 'About the Teeth of Sharks' from *You Read to Me, I'll Read to You* (HarperCollins*Publishers*), by permission of Myra Ciardi for the Ciardi Family Publishing Trust. **Leonard Clark**: 'Mushrooms', first published in *Six of the Best: A Puffin Sextet of Poets* chosen by Anne Harvey (Puffin 1989), by permission of Robert A. Clark. **Frank Collymore**: 'Spider', by permission of Ellice Collymore. **Stanley Cook**: 'Bluebells' from *The Squirrel in Town* (Blackie, 1988), copyright © Estate of Stanley Cook, by permission of Sarah Matthews. **Wendy Cope**: 'Huff', copyright © Wendy Cope, by permission of the author. **Roald Dahl**: 'Aunt Sponge and Aunt Spiker' from *James and the Giant Peach* (Puffin, 1961), by permission of David Higham Associates. **Walter de la Mare**: 'The Listeners' from *The Complete Poems of Walter de la Mare* (1969), by permission of The Literary Trustees of Walter de la Mare, and the Society of Authors as their representatives. **Berlie Doherty**: 'I'm Frightened in Dark Caves' from *Walking on Air* (Walker Books), by permission of David Higham Associates. **Carol Ann Duffy**: 'Chocs' from *Meeting Midnight* (2000), by permission of the publishers, Faber & Faber Ltd. **Michael Dugan**: 'Misnomer' from *Flocks's Socks and Other Shocks* (Penguin Australia), by permission of the author. **Richard Edwards**: 'The Rainflower' from *The Word Party* (Lutterworth, 1986), by permission of the author. **T. S. Eliot**: 'The song of the Jellicles' from *Old Possum's Book of Practical Cats* (1939), by permission of the publishers, Faber & Faber Ltd. **Gavin Ewart**: 'The Weather' first published in *The Oxford Treasury of Children's Poems* edited by Michael Harrison & Christopher Stuart-Clark (Oxford University Press 1988), by permission of Mrs Margo Ewart. **Eleanor Farjeon**: 'Zodiac' from *The Children's Bells* (Oxford University Press 1957), by permission of David Higham Associates. **Max Fatchen**: '"Jump Over the Moon?" the Cow Declared' from *Songs for My Dog and Other People* (Kestrel, 1980), by permission of John Johnson (Authors' Agent) Ltd. **Rachel Field**: 'Something Told the Wild Geese' from *Poems*, copyright © 1934 Macmillan Publishing Company, copyright © renewed 1962 by Arthur S. Pederson, by permission of Simon & Schuster Books for Young Readers, an imprint of Simon & Schuster Children's Publishing Division. **Aileen Fisher**: 'Christmas Secrets' from *Out in the Dark and Daylight* (Harper & Row 1980), copyright © 1980 by Aileen Fisher, by permission of Marian Reiner on behalf of the author. **Roy Fuller**: 'Horrible Things' from *The World Through the Window* (Blackie 1989), by permission of John Fuller. **Rose Fyleman**: 'Witch, Witch' from *Fifty One New Nursery Rhymes* (Methuen/Doubleday 1931), by permission of the Society of Authors as the Literary Representative of the Estate of Rose Fyleman. **Nikki Giovanni**: 'mattie lou at twelve' from *Spin a Soft Black Song* (revised edition), copyright © 1971, 1985 by Nikki Giovanni, by permission of the publisher, Farrar, Straus & Giroux, LLC. **Grace Walker Gordon**: 'The Sprat and the Jackfish' from *Sunsong 1* edited by Pamela Mordecai and Grace Walker Gordon (Longman Jamaica, 1984), by permission of the author. **Kenneth Grahame**: 'A Song for Toad' from *The Wind in the Willows* (Methuen, 1928), copyright © The University Chest, Oxford, by permission of Curtis Brown Ltd, London. **Robert Graves**: 'The Penny Fiddle' from *Robert Graves: Complete Poems* (Carcanet Press Ltd, 2000), by permission of the publishers.